I0817407

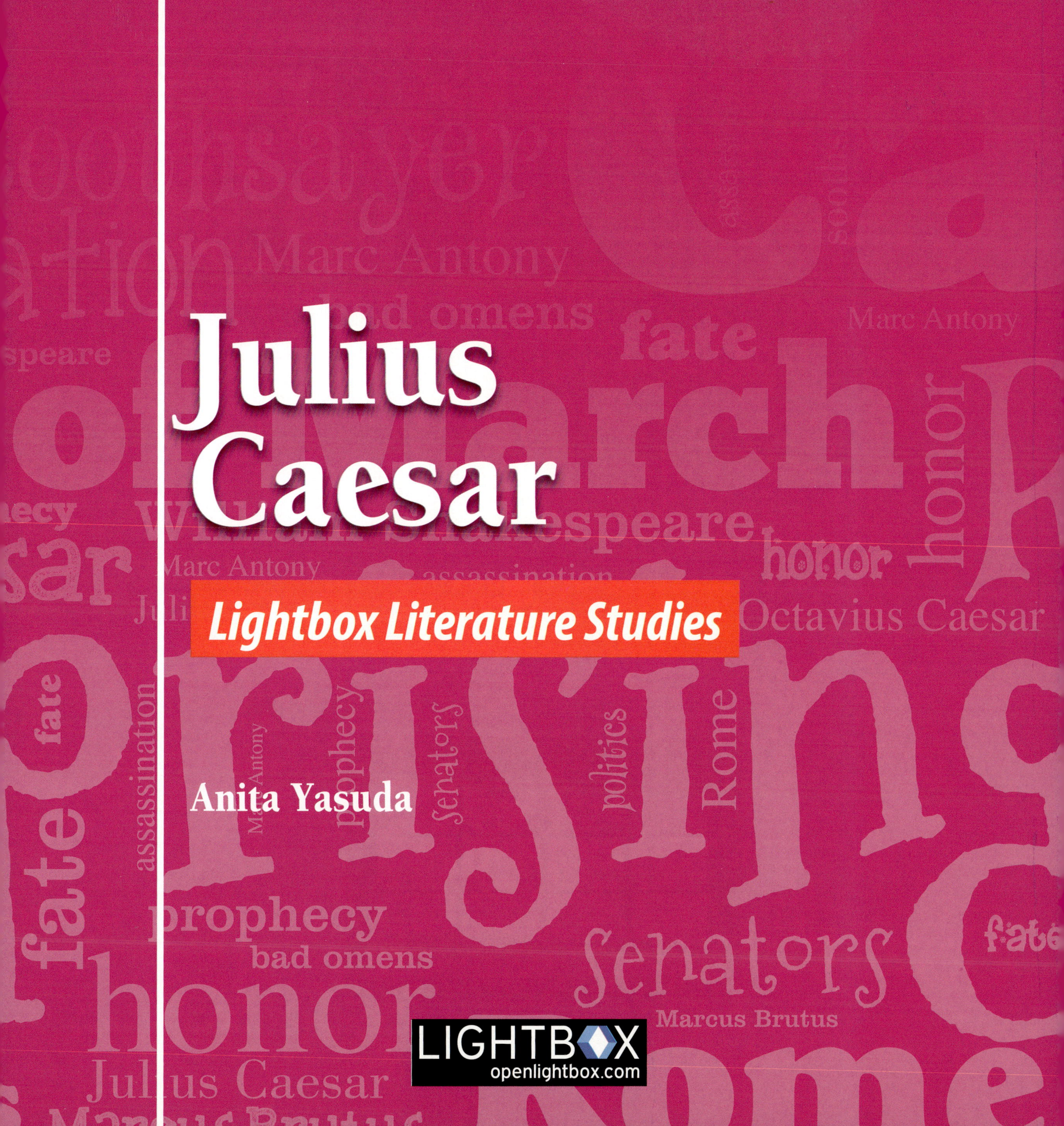

Julius Caesar
Lightbox Literature Studies
Anita Yasuda
LIGHTBOX
openlightbox.com

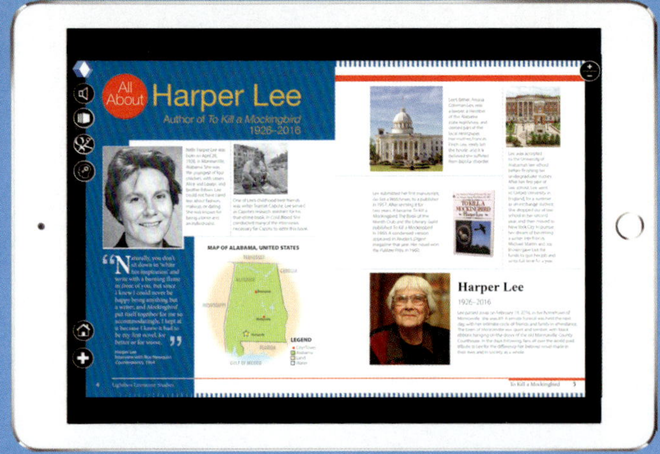


Lightbox is an all-inclusive digital solution for the teaching and learning of curriculum topics in an original, groundbreaking way. Lightbox is based on National Curriculum Standards.

## STANDARD FEATURES OF LIGHTBOX

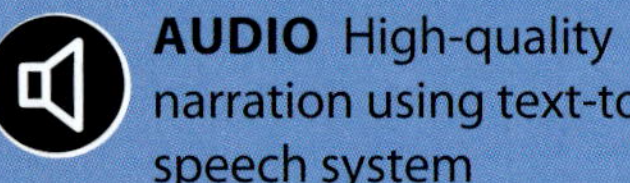
**AUDIO** High-quality narration using text-to-speech system

**VIDEOS** Embedded high-definition video clips

**ACTIVITIES** Printable PDFs that can be emailed and graded

**WEBLINKS** Curated links to external, child-safe resources

**SLIDESHOWS** Pictorial overviews of key concepts

**TRANSPARENCIES** Step-by-step layering of maps, diagrams, charts, and timelines

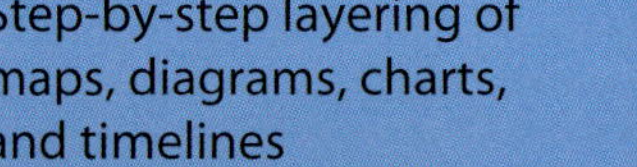

**INTERACTIVE MAPS** Interactive maps and aerial satellite imagery

**QUIZZES** Ten multiple choice questions that are automatically graded and emailed for teacher assessment

**KEY WORDS** Matching key concepts to their definitions

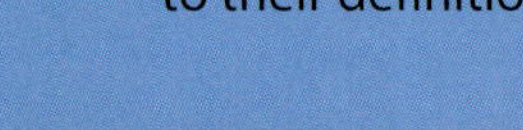

**MORE** Extra information and details on the subject

**FIRST HAND** Letters, diaries, and other primary sources

**DOCS** Speeches, newspaper articles, and other historical documents

# Contents

RSC
It MUST be by his DEATH
William Shakespeare
JULIUS CAESAR
EDITED BY JONATHAN BATE AND ERIC RASMUSSEN

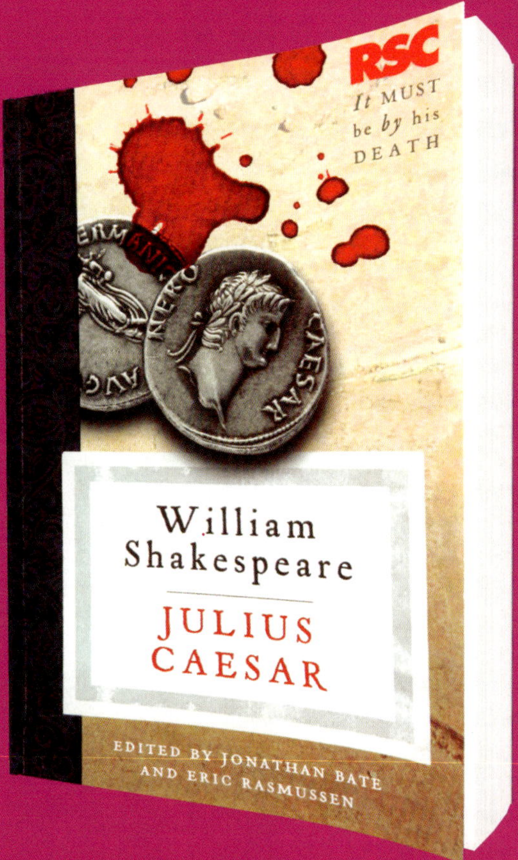

**EXTENSION ACTIVITY**

## Conducting an Interview

**Students will conduct an interview with a community member about a time period in their community's history, and submit an audio recording and transcript of the interview. An exemplary interview will meet the following criteria.**

- Clearly defines the purpose of the interview
- Conducts thorough background research to inform the focus of the interview and the questions
- Drafts a complete list of thoughtful, in-depth, and varied questions prior to the interview
- Interviews a subject with relevant knowledge on the topic and time period in question
- Asks questions in a logical order, building upon each other
- Treats the interview subject in a polite, respectful, and professional manner
- Does not interrupt or rush the interview subject
- Shows interest and enthusiasm in responses and follow-up questions
- Chooses follow-up questions that demonstrate active listening
- Asks for clarification and further details when necessary
- Asks questions about personal experiences related to the topic
- Asks questions regarding factual information and the interview subject's opinion on the topic
- Asks creative questions that reflect fresh insights on the topic
- Records the full interview in a quiet environment
- Organizes and edits the interview transcript to be clear and factual

# William Shakespeare

## Author of *Julius Caesar*
## 1564–1616

William Shakespeare was born in 1564, in Stratford-upon-Avon, England. His father, John Shakespeare, was a successful glove maker who also held various public offices. His mother, Mary, was from a respectable land-owning family. Shakespeare had five younger siblings.

There are no records of Shakespeare attending school, but historians assume that he attended the King's New School in Stratford. Boys from the middle class usually attended grammar school from the ages of about 7 to 14. Students at this time studied Latin and the works of classical authors.

> "All the world's a stage, And all the men and women merely players; They have their exits and their entrances, And one man in his time plays many parts, His acts being seven ages."
>
> William Shakespeare, *As You Like It*, Act 2, Scene 7

### MAP OF THE UNITED KINGDOM

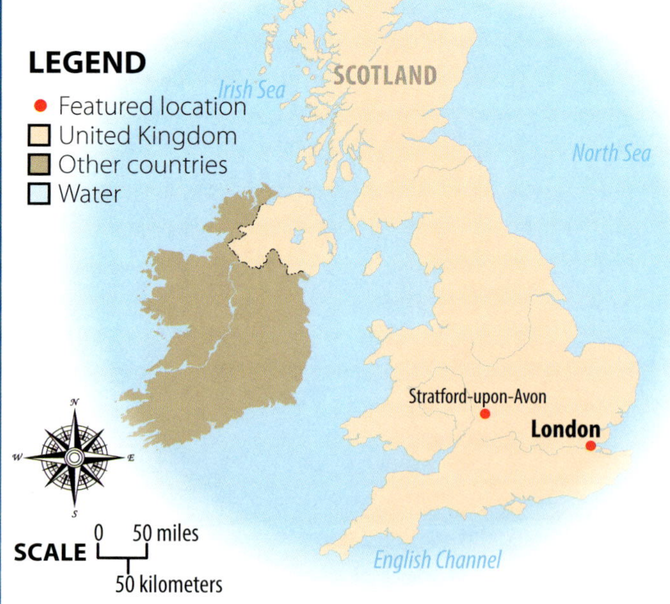

It is not known when Shakespeare left grammar school. He married Anne Hathaway in 1582, and the couple had three children. From 1585 to 1592, nothing is known about Shakespeare's life. Historians call this period his "lost years." Some historians speculate that Shakespeare may have taught at this time. It is also believed he may have joined a theatrical company in his hometown of Stratford.

Shakespeare began working in London as an actor and a playwright around 1592. He wrote approximately 37 plays before 1613, including some of his best-known comedies and tragedies. He also wrote poems and sonnets. His first play, *Henry VI, Part One*, was first performed around 1592. Throughout the 1590s, interest in his plays increased. He became part owner of a theatrical company in London called the Lord Chamberlain's Men.

In 1599, the Lord Chamberlain's Men moved to a new public playhouse on London's South Bank. It was a round wooden theater called the Globe. The theater's three tiers of galleries could fit an audience of 3,000 people. At this time, Shakespeare wrote a new play that was performed on the Globe's stage. The play was a tragedy called *The Tragedy of Julius Caesar*. According to reports from the time, actors wore elaborate costumes on a bare stage with few props.

Shakespeare died at the age of 52 on April 23, 1616. He bequeathed most of his estate to his daughter, Susanna, with a smaller allowance for his wife. He also left money to three associates, Richard Burbage, Henry Condell, and John Hemminge, whom he had worked with throughout his career. Immediately after his death, there were few tributes to him. Historians speculate this may be because Shakespeare had retired from the stage years earlier. In 1623, Shakespeare's friends and colleagues arranged for his plays to be printed in a single volume, the *First Folio*. The forward of the *First Folio* contains a tribute to the greatness of Shakespeare's work.

## TEACHER NOTES

### Google Maps

**Shakespeare's Birthplace, Stratford-upon-Avon, Warwickshire, England**

Explore Shakespeare's hometown using the street view of his birthplace, now a heritage site, and the surrounding streets of Stratford-upon-Avon.

### First Hand

***Shakespeare in the Park's Gregg Henry on Playing a Very Trumpian Julius Caesar***

Examine a May 2017 interview with actor Gregg Henry about his performance as the title character in the Delacorte Theater's production of *Julius Caesar*.

1. Many people have drawn comparisons between Julius Caesar and U.S. President Donald Trump, especially due to this particular portrayal of the character, who is costumed in a suit and tie, and fluffy blonde wig, much like the president. How does Henry describe what it is like to play a so-called "Trumpian" version of Caesar? In what ways are the two figures similar? How do they differ?
2. How do the themes of the play relate to the current political climate of the United States? Do you think this approach to the play and its title character is appropriate? Why or why not? Give reasons for your answer.

**EXTENSION ACTIVITY**

### Researching for a Writing Assignment

**Students will complete a thorough research process to prepare for a writing assignment, and organize their research in a logical manner that supports their writing. An exemplary research process will meet the following criteria.**

- Creates a goal for the research, based on the topic and working thesis
- Creates specific, thoughtful, and inventive research questions that are relevant to the topic of the writing assignment
- Produces a list of categories, key words, and related ideas to effectively assist in researching
- Uses high-quality sources that pertain to the topic and come in a variety of formats, such as books, journals, primary sources, websites, and databases
- Determines accuracy of all sources
- Uses sources that provide balanced research and various perspectives on the topic in question
- Takes notes to highlight the key facts and ideas in order to answer all research questions
- Extracts relevant, detailed information from the sources during the note-taking process
- Organizes the research notes in a clear and concise manner
- Organizes the research notes logically and in a way that sets up the information and ideas for analysis and the writing process
- Analyzes the information and produces ideas and points to support the working thesis
- Uses an effective and suitable format to present all research
- Properly cites all sources used

# Setting of the Play

Shakespeare set *The Tragedy of Julius Caesar* in Ancient Rome, a city that is now the capital of Italy. Rome was once the central city of a huge empire, stretching from North Africa and the Mediterranean Sea to Europe. Shakespeare's knowledge of Rome may have come from history texts written by classical authors such as Livy and Ovid. He also drew inspiration from Greek historian Plutarch's *The Lives of the Noble Greeks and Romans*.

## Snapshot

### Rome in the First Century BC

**100 BC** Gaius Julius Caesar is born

**49 BC** Caesar's army defeats that of his rival Pompey

**44 BC** Caesar is assassinated by his opponents

### Shakespeare's Rome

"None that I know will be, much that I fear may chance.
Good morrow to you. Here the street is narrow:
The throng that follows Caesar at the heels,
Of senators, of praetors, common suitors,
Will crowd a feeble man almost to death:
I'll get me to a place more void, and there
Speak to great Caesar as he comes along."

Soothsayer, Act 2, Scene 6

In 2013, the Chicago Shakespeare Theater contemporized *Julius Caesar*. In this interpretation of the play, the director reimagined it as a coup against an American president. Instead of Ancient Rome, the set designer created a backdrop reminiscent of a presidential inauguration in Washington, D.C. Senator characters dressed in business suits and carried cell phones. The army did not look like a Roman legion, but wore modern fatigues, and paratroopers descended onto the stage.

Shakespeare chose the steps of the Roman Senate building as the location for Caesar's assassination. Assassins killed the actual Caesar at Pompey's Theater. It no longer exists, but there is a square in Rome called Largo de Torre Argentina where it once stood. The 2013 stage adaptation modernized the classical Roman architecture of the Senate with the addition of a contemporary political campaign banner. After Caesar's assassination in the play, graffiti appears on the marble columns used in the inauguration scene.

## TEACHER NOTES

### Video

**The great conspiracy against Julius Caesar - Kathryn Tempest**
Find out more about Caesar's assassination by watching this video.

1. Why did the Liberators want Caesar dead?
2. Why did Marc Antony give a speech at Caesar's funeral? What were the effects of this speech?
3. Why did Brutus, whose own life had been saved by Caesar, join in the plot to assassinate him? Do you see Brutus as a selfless fighter against dictatorship or an opportunistic traitor? Why? Compare and contrast these two interpretations and give evidence to support your opinion.

### Weblink

**Julius Caesar**
Learn more about the life and times of Julius Caesar by reading this article.

1. Why did Caesar break off his engagement to a plebeian girl to marry Cornelia? How did this change Caesar's position?
2. Why do you think Caesar disobeyed orders to return to Rome? His crossing of the Rubicon River was considered an act of war. Do you think this was deliberate? Why or why not? How did this decision shape the events that unfolded next?
3. The article claims that Octavian, Caesar's adopted heir, "...initiated the end of the Roman Republic and the beginning of the Roman Empire." Do you agree with this assertion? Why or why not? Explain your answer.

## EXTENSION ACTIVITY

### Analyzing Bias in a Document

**Students will analyze the bias that exists in a document from a different historical time and place, and how that bias shapes the opinions presented in the document. An exemplary analysis of bias in a document will meet the following criteria.**

- Identifies the main points presented in the document
- Offers an in-depth interpretation of the document
- Differentiates between facts and opinions
- Identifies the writer
- Presents information about the writer
- Assesses the writer's reliability
- Determines the goals for the document
- Considers and assesses the writer's perspective
- Determines the writer's intended audience
- Identifies when and where the document was written
- Describes the historical context for the time and place in which the document was created, and analyzes how this context might have shaped the opinions expressed in the document
- Infers political or societal influences that may have shaped the opinions presented in the document
- Determines whether the writer had first-hand knowledge of the topic or event, or whether they are reporting as a secondary source
- Determines the document's bias
- Infers what interests the writer might have had that led them to create this document
- Explores other sources related to the topic of the document

# Time Period of the Play

*The Tragedy of Julius Caesar* is set around 44 BC. The play begins after Caesar, a powerful general, is elected to the highest office in the Roman Empire. At this time, the government of Rome was a republic, with elected officials and shared power between different branches to prevent one individual from becoming too powerful. However, the legislative branch, called the Senate, was **corrupt**. Senators from the wealthy land-owning class were more concerned with personal gain than with the welfare of the Empire. As the Roman Empire grew, it became more difficult for the government to control.

These excerpts from the play show how Mark Antony plans to purge the Senate of opposition after he has assumed power.

### The Roman Empire

"He shall not live. Look, with a spot I damn him.
But, Lepidus, go you to Caesar's house.
Fetch the will hither, and we shall determine
How to cut off some charge in legacies."

Mark Antony, Act 4, Scene 1

"And now, Octavius, Listen great things.
Brutus and Cassius Are levying powers.
We must straight make head.
Therefore let our alliance be combined,
Our best friends made, our means stretched."

Mark Antony, Act 4, Scene 1

Julius Caesar was a brilliant military commander. He rose to power during the Great Roman Civil War (49–45 BC). After he had taken charge, Caesar wanted to strengthen Rome's control over its empire. He encouraged Roman citizens to settle in colonies to help spread Roman **influence**. Believing that Rome needed a centralized government, Caesar appointed himself dictator for life, and some senators feared that Rome would become a monarchy again. These senators assassinated Caesar in 44 BC, believing that his death would restore the Republic. Their motivations for killing Caesar became the focus of Shakespeare's play.

After Caesar's death, Mark Antony, Lepidus, and Octavius formed a political alliance called the Second Triumvirate. Each man controlled a different part of the empire. Two of Caesar's assassins, Brutus and Cassius, did not agree with this arrangement. Their legions attacked the Triumvirate, but were defeated. After this defeat, each member of the Triumvirate fought for sole control of the empire, which is where Shakespeare's play ends.

After forming the Second Triumvirate, Mark Antony, Lepidus, and Octavius created a list of Roman senators whom they believed were a threat to their power. From this, the Triumvirate had 300 senators and 2,000 people from noble families put to death. Shakespeare refers to this list in Act 4 of *Julius Caesar*.

## TEACHER NOTES

### Video

**The Roman Empire. Or Republic. Or...Which Was It?: Crash Course World History #10**
Discover how the Roman Republic became the Roman Empire and what role Caesar played by watching this video.

1. Why was Caesar considered the "undisputed master of Rome"? What reforms did he pursue? How did these reforms strengthen his power?
2. Why did the conspirators think Caesar's death would bring about the restoration of the Roman Republic? What actually happened instead? Why?

### Document

***What the Romans did for Shakespeare: Rome and Roman values in Shakespeare's plays***
Examine the article by Andrew Dickson published on March 15, 2016 about the influence of classical civilization and literature on Shakespeare, and the playwright's critique of Roman values.

1. What are the main points of the article and how are they presented? Are these points conveyed effectively to the reader? Explain why you think so.
2. What conclusions does Dickson draw in this article? Do you agree or disagree with him? Why? Support your answer.

**EXTENSION ACTIVITY**

## Writing a Short Story

**Students will choose an excerpt from the play and use it as their inspiration in writing a short story. An exemplary short story will meet the following criteria.**

- Engages the reader from the opening line
- Establishes a clear, consistent point of view
- Introduces a narrator and a setting
- Develops an engaging conflict at the heart of the narrative to build tension and keep the reader interested
- Develops characters and events through purposeful and well-crafted literary devices
- Creates a logical progression of events in the narrative that build upon each other using various techniques
- Explores ideas, concepts, and writing styles with creativity and originality
- Demonstrates a high level of skill in using appropriate narrative techniques to tell the story
- Concludes the narrative in a thoughtful, effective manner appropriate to the narrative
- Uses varied, purposeful diction and syntax to affect style and serve the narrative
- Writes with clarity, imagination, and a unique, personal voice
- Does not use stereotypes or clichés
- Uses effective, believable dialogue
- Uses correct spelling, grammar, and punctuation

# Conflict in the Play

Conflict in literature is a struggle between two opposing forces. For a protagonist to resolve this conflict, they face many challenges. Sometimes, these challenges come from within, forcing characters to question their actions and motivations. Conflict may also come from other characters, society as a whole, or nature. Authors use conflict to create tension and move the story towards its conclusion.

## The Four Major Types of Conflict in Literature

MAN vs. MAN

Man versus man is a popular type of conflict in fiction. The protagonist must struggle against the actions of the antagonist to reach his or her goal. Sometimes, it is a struggle between good and evil. In *Percy Jackson and the Olympians: The Lightning Thief*, Percy has to battle Luke, who is helping Kronos to overthrow the Olympians, to return Zeus's lightning bolt.

MAN vs. SELF

In a man versus self conflict, the protagonist struggles with a major decision. This decision has important consequences, which may influence both the protagonist's life and the lives of others. In *Macbeth*, the title character becomes deeply disturbed after he decides to murder the king of Scotland. Macbeth cannot stop thinking about what he has done.

MAN vs. SOCIETY

This conflict is based on the protagonist's beliefs. The character does not agree with the beliefs or actions of a group, and faces challenges from a group or society as a whole. In the novel *The Help*, Skeeter stands up to racism in her hometown of Jackson, Mississippi, in the 1960s. Skeeter collects stories from the town's maids to show how their employers mistreat them terribly.

MAN vs. NATURE

In a man versus nature conflict, the protagonist must overcome a natural obstacle, such as a storm, a mountain, or an entire landscape. In the film *The Martian*, Mark Watney struggles to survive on Mars. After Watney's mission goes wrong, the crew, believing that Watney is dead, leaves him behind. Now stranded on the planet's surface, he must face fierce sand storms and the threat of starvation until help arrives.

# Types of Conflict in *Julius Caesar*

The two main types of conflict in *The Tragedy of Julius Caesar* are man versus self and man versus society. These conflicts drive the major events of the play towards its climax.

## Man versus Self

"Since Cassius first did whet me against Caesar,
I have not slept.
Between the acting of a dreadful thing
And the first motion, all the interim is
Like a phantasma, or a hideous dream:
The Genius and the mortal instruments
Are then in council; and the state of man,
Like to a little kingdom, suffers then
The nature of an insurrection."

Marcus Brutus, Act 2, Scene 1

## Man versus Society

"O you hard hearts, you cruel men of Rome,
Knew you not Pompey? Many a time and oft
Have you climbed up to walls and battlements,
To towers and windows, yea, to chimney tops,
You infants in your arms, and there have sat
The livelong day, with patient expectation,
To see great Pompey pass the streets of Rome.
And when you saw his chariot but appear,
Have you not made an universal shout,
That Tiber trembled underneath her banks
To hear the replication of your sounds
Made in her concave shores?
And do you now put on your best attire?
And do you now cull out a holiday?
And do you now strew flowers in his way
That comes in triumph over Pompey's blood?
Be gone!"

Marullus, Act 1, Scene 1

## TEACHER NOTES

### More

**The Types of Conflict in *Julius Caesar***

Analyze the excerpts from the play revealing the types of conflict as they appear in *Julius Caesar*.

1. How do these excerpts of conflict reveal the play's theme? How do they reveal character? Explain and defend your ideas.
2. Write an analysis of Shakespeare's development of conflict between Brutus and Caesar. What deeper truths may be suggested about these characters as a result of their conflict?

### Weblink

**Elements of Drama: Conflict**

Examine the blog post about conflict in theater.

1. Who is the intended audience for this blog post? Is the tone and language used appropriate for this audience? Why or why not?
2. What are the writer's goals and how does he attempt to accomplish them? How successful is he? Why do you think so?
3. Compare and contrast internal conflict with external conflict. In what ways are they similar? How do they differ? Give specific examples of each type of conflict. These can be from plays, novels, short stories, films, or television shows.

**EXTENSION ACTIVITY**

### Analyzing a Video

**Students will watch and assess a video related to a component of the play, and write an analysis of the video. An exemplary video analysis will meet the following criteria.**

- Identifies the purpose of the video
- Identifies the intended audience of the video
- Describes how the content of the video is presented
- Summarizes the information and opinions presented in the video
- Analyzes the quality of the content presented in the video
- Assesses the effectiveness of the video
- Discusses the technical aspects of the video and whether or not these enhance the content
- Determines whether the images and graphics used in the video relate to the content
- Determines whether the video is easy to follow and understand
- Gives the analysis a clear and consistent purpose
- Organizes the analysis in a logical, effective manner
- Presents a strong, clear argument about the video
- Provides strong and accurate details to support the argument about the video
- Considers other perspectives on the purpose and effectiveness of the video
- Makes connections between the video and the play
- Properly integrates quotations from the video
- Cites all sources used in the analysis

# Introducing the Characters

To develop a character's personality, writers convey information through indirect and direct methods. This process is called characterization. Writers might reveal the personality of a character through his or her actions, thoughts, or speech. A character may also be developed through his or her mannerisms or looks. Authors may even have another character in the story reveal how he or she feels about the character. They may also choose to reveal a character's traits from the perspective of another character.

## Major Characters in *Julius Caesar*

**Julius Caesar**
The title character of the play and new military leader of Rome ignores warnings about his safety, perhaps due to arrogance.

**Mark Antony**
The play's antagonist and Caesar's friend uses his skill as an orator at Caesar's public funeral to encourage the crowd to rebel.

**Marcus Brutus**
The play's protagonist is an idealistic politician who is **manipulated** into betraying Caesar.

**Caius Cassius**
The instigator of the **conspiracy** against Caesar is a general who convinces Brutus that Caesar is a tyrant.

**Calpurnia**
Julius Caesar's wife believes in bad omens and warns her husband not to go to the Senate on the Ides of March.

Two of the most important characters in a narrative are the protagonist and the antagonist. These characters are essential to the plot because, together, they build tension in the story. The protagonist is the main character in a story. He or she encounters problems or conflicts through the course of the story, which need to be solved. Marcus Brutus is the protagonist in *Julius Caesar*. Brutus has the respect of the Senate and the people, but he is an idealist. This flaw leads Brutus to struggle with his vision for the Roman Republic, and ultimately, **betray** Caesar.

The antagonist is a character that stands in the way of the goals of the protagonist. He or she is not necessarily a bad person. The antagonist may have a different set of goals, or may act against the protagonist due to a misunderstanding. In *Julius Caesar*, Mark Antony is the antagonist. After Caesar is murdered, Mark Antony encourages the Romans to turn on Caesar's assassins and drive them from Rome.

Writers introduce a variety of minor characters to keep the plot moving forward or to support the story's main characters. Cassius is an example of a dynamic character because he changes as the story unfolds. In contrast, Casca is a static character, as he does not change over the course of the story. A flat character, such as Julius Caesar, has one distinguishing characteristic, while a rounded character, such as Mark Antony, has many qualities and his or her own goals.

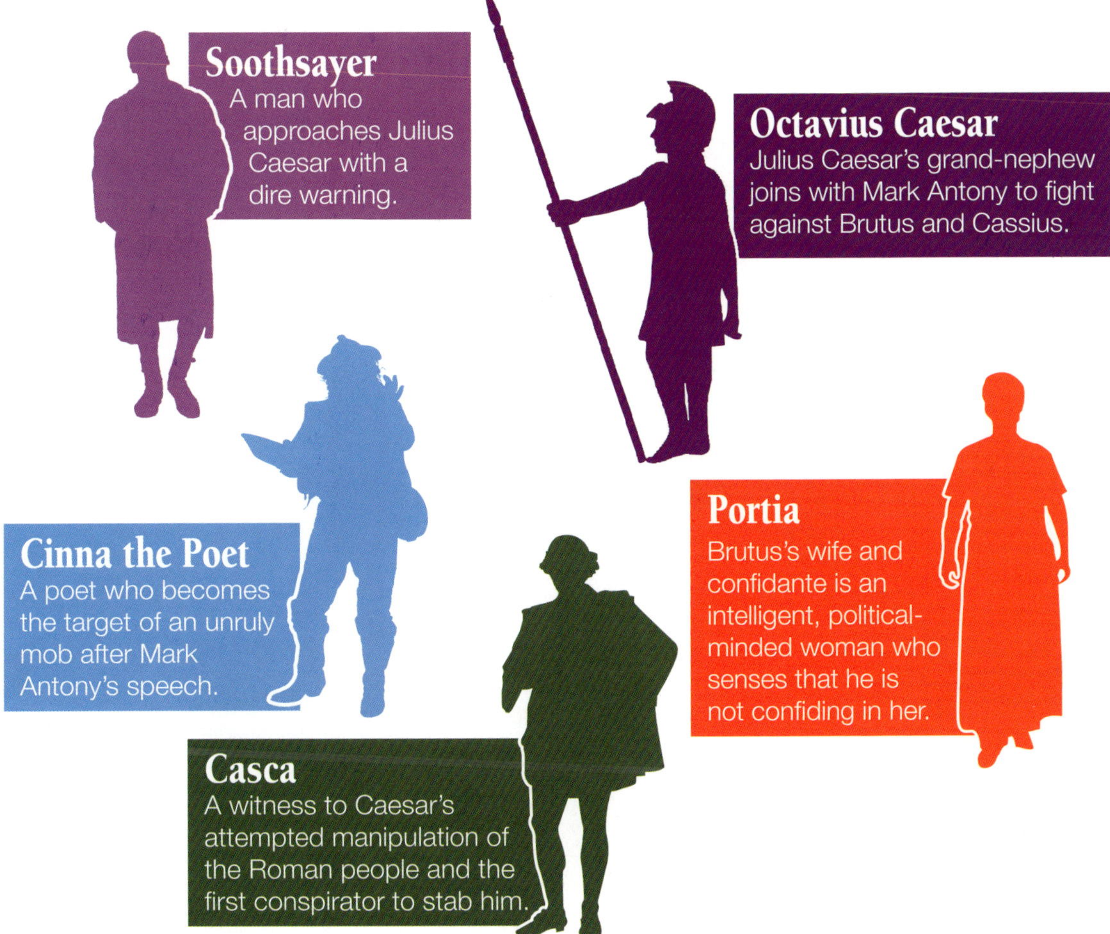

## TEACHER NOTES

### Video

**Video SparkNotes: Shakespeare's Julius Caesar summary**

Learn more about *Julius Caesar* by watching this video.

1. Why does Cassius need Brutus in order to pull off Caesar's assassination? How does he attempt to manipulate Brutus? What might have happened if Brutus had refused to go along with the conspiracy?
2. Do you think that Caesar's fate was predetermined? Why or why not? Give evidence to support your position.

### More

**Character Development in *Julius Caesar***

Analyze the characters in *Julius Caesar* using the descriptions on the character map and excerpts from each character. Then, choose a character and answer the following questions.

1. Which of the writer's techniques are most effective at revealing this character's traits? Why?
2. In what ways is the characterization of this character ineffective? What could be done to improve this character's function in the play? Defend your ideas with evidence.

EXTENSION ACTIVITY

### Creating a Literary Device Analysis Booklet

**Students will analyze the author's use of a literary device in the play, and create a booklet to present this analysis. An exemplary literary device analysis booklet will meet the following criteria.**

- Defines the chosen literary device accurately and in detail
- Places the definition of the literary device at the beginning of the booklet
- Provides strong, specific examples of how this literary device is used in the play
- Describes examples in detail, with quotations properly integrated
- Includes thorough analysis of the use, purpose, and effectiveness of each example of how the chosen literary device is used in the play
- Arranges all pages logically
- Examples are organized chronologically
- Provides no more than one example and its analysis per page
- Creates a neat, well-organized, and attractive booklet
- Booklet is colorful and displays the student's creativity
- Uses illustrations to represent the chosen literary device and the examples of how it is used in the play

# The Art of Storytelling

Storytelling is a way to entertain or engage listeners. A story can teach **values** and history, or it may communicate perspectives on a society. A narrative, or story, is a series of events logically arranged by the author. A writer creates stories by purposefully organizing the narrative to build toward a satisfying conclusion. The writer can also use a number of literary devices to create a distinct style and to convey the narrative's overall message. To tell his story effectively, Shakespeare organized his narrative, created a plot, and used literary devices in *The Tragedy of Julius Caesar*.

## Structure of a Narrative

Each narrative has a structure, which writers keep in mind when creating a story. The most common narrative structure, known as dramatic structure or Freytag's Pyramid, consists of five main components, which are all used in *Julius Caesar*.

### Freytag's Pyramid

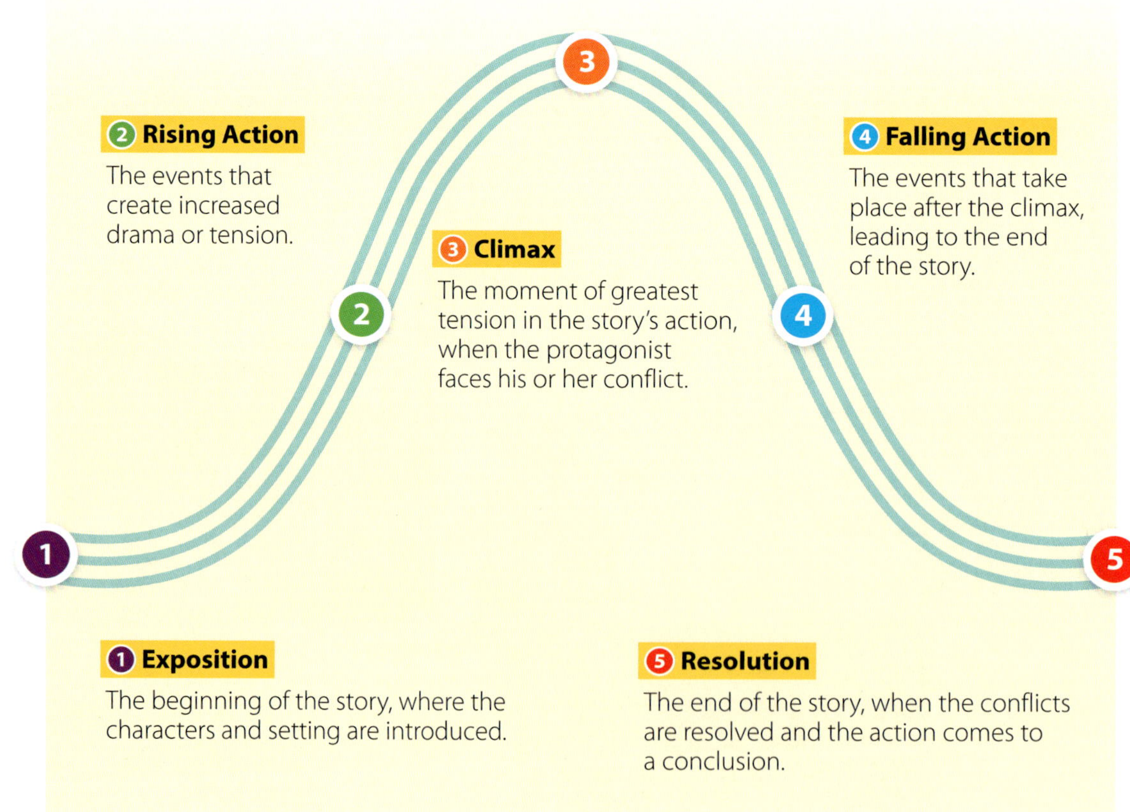

## Plot

Every narrative needs to have a plot. Plot is the series of actions that propel the story forward. The plotline is the order in which events, or plot points, take place from beginning to end. These events build on each other and are organized in a logical manner, creating the narrative.

### Plot Points in Act 1 of *Julius Caesar*

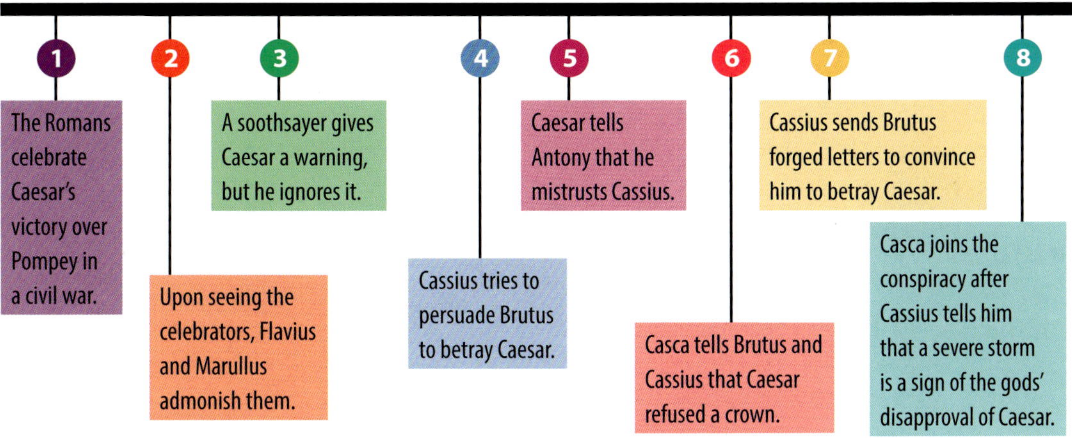


## Literary Devices

A literary device is any particular feature of a work of literature that can be identified, studied, and analyzed. There are two types of literary devices. These are literary elements and literary techniques.

**TEACHER NOTES**

**Weblink**

**Literary Devices**
Find out more about literary elements and literary techniques.

1. What is the difference between a literary element and a literary technique? Explain in your own words, using examples from *Julius Caesar*.
2. What are the functions of literary devices? How do they contribute to a reader's overall experience, understanding, and enjoyment of a literary work?

**More**

**Examples of Literary Techniques from the Play**
Analyze the author's use of literary techniques and how they contribute to the narrative of *Julius Caesar*.

1. Choose one literary technique used in the play. In what particular way did the author use this literary technique? How effective was its usage?
2. What arguments can be made for the use of your chosen literary technique in a text? If this technique were overused or underutilized, what effect might it have on an author's work?

**EXTENSION ACTIVITY**

### Analyzing a Newspaper Article

**Students will assess a newspaper article and write an analysis. An exemplary analysis will meet the following criteria.**

- Identifies the topic of the article
- Identifies the main points and opinions presented in the article
- Identifies the writer of the article
- Presents information about the writer and infers how his or her life may have shaped this opinion
- Assesses the writer's reliability
- Analyzes how the writer makes his or her argument
- Uses evidence from the article to show how the writer supports his or her argument
- Analyzes the writer's use of literary devices to enhance the article
- Differentiates between the facts and opinions presented in the article
- Identifies when and where the article was published, and determines its intended audience
- Identifies and understands the goals of the article
- Assesses the effectiveness of the format (a newspaper opinion article) in presenting the writer's argument
- Connects the article to the societal and historical context in which it was written
- Infers what is not said about this topic in the article
- Identifies what information is unintentionally implied in the article
- Infers what other opinions may be presented about this topic and who may be most likely to express them
- Uses a number of other resources to analyze the context of the article

# Theme in the Play

A dramatist develops his or her plays with a theme in mind. A theme is an idea or belief. This may be a view of life that people of all cultures, age groups, and backgrounds can understand. A writer can express a theme by creatively weaving it into a play.

Sometimes, a play's theme contains a moral message about how people should behave. Characters learn these lessons through interactions with other characters. Dramatists do not always clearly state the theme, and it is common for themes to be suggested. It is then up to the viewer to think about the play's message and arrive at his or her own conclusions about the theme.

## Values

Closely related to the play's themes are the values held by the play's characters. Dramatists construct characters who reveal different values through mannerisms, dialogue, and actions. In some cases, a character's values will reflect those of the writer. Sometimes, these values help to develop a play's theme.

## Major Themes of *Julius Caesar*

Shakespeare drew on a critical event from Ancient Rome to create a tragic play about Julius Caesar. By focusing on the actions, conflicts, and motivations of the characters, he developed the play's central theme of the corrupting nature of power. Themes of human fallibility, fate and free will, and personal versus public interest are also present in the play.

### Power and Corruption

"Th' abuse of greatness is when it disjoins
Remorse from power. And, to speak truth
of Caesar,
I have not known when his affections swayed
More than his reason. But 'tis a common proof
That lowliness is young **ambition**'s ladder,
Whereto the climber upward turns his face.
But when he once attains the upmost round,
He then unto the ladder turns his back..."

Marcus Brutus, Act 2, Scene 1

Marcus Brutus

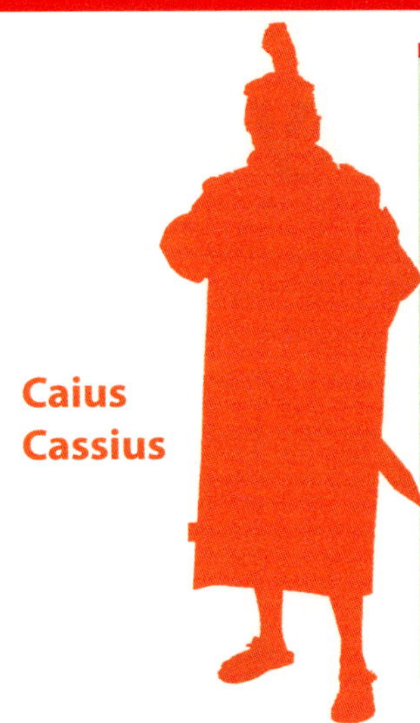


## Fate and Free Will

"Why, man, he doth bestride the narrow world
Like a Colossus, and we petty men
Walk under his huge legs and peep about
To find ourselves dishonorable graves.
Men at some time are masters of their fates.
The fault, dear Brutus, is not in our stars
But in ourselves, that we are underlings."

Caius Cassius, Act 1, Scene 1

## Personal versus Public Interest

"The cause is in my will. I will not come.
That is enough to satisfy the senate.
But for your private satisfaction,
Because I love you, I will let you know.
Calpurnia here, my wife, stays me at home.
She dreamt tonight she saw my statue,
Which, like a fountain with an hundred spouts,
Did run pure blood. And many lusty Romans
Came smiling and did bathe their hands in it.
And these does she apply for warnings and portents
And evils imminent, and on her knee
Hath begged that I will stay at home today."

Julius Caesar, Act 2, Scene 2

## Secondary Themes

A writer does not emphasize a secondary theme as much because it is not as important as the central theme. However, although a secondary theme plays a lesser role, it adds another layer to the ideas presented. This makes the story more complex and allows for deeper literary analysis. **Loyalty**, friendship, jealousy, and the power of language or **rhetoric** are all examples of secondary themes in *Julius Caesar*.

**TEACHER NOTES**

### Weblink

***Why Power Corrupts***

Evaluate the October 2012 *Smithsonian Magazine* article discussing why power brings out the best in some people and the worst in others.

1. According to the study, "power doesn't corrupt; it heightens pre-existing ethical tendencies." Explain in your own words what this means. What are the implications of this conclusion?
2. How does this study apply to *Julius Caesar*? What can you say about the title character and his quest for power, given the conclusion of this study?

### More

**Major and Secondary Themes**

Analyze the author's development of themes over the course of the play.

1. Choose a secondary theme from this spread and analyze its appearances in the play. How does this theme first emerge? Which is the most poignant example of this theme in the play?
2. What particular commentary might the author be making about life as a result of this theme's presence in the text? Explain and defend your ideas.
3. Choose a major theme presented on pages 16–17. In what ways does your chosen secondary theme relate to this major theme? Does it deepen or detract from the major theme? How or in what way?

**EXTENSION ACTIVITY**

### Creating a Symbolism Poster

**Students will choose one of the other symbols listed on page 19 and analyze its role in the play. They will then create a poster to present their analysis. An exemplary symbolism poster will meet the following criteria.**

- Presents a clear purpose that is conveyed throughout the poster
- Shows an understanding of the concept of symbolism and the role it has in the play
- Provides an in-depth analysis of what the symbol represents
- Discusses the role the symbol has in the play
- Clearly indicates where the symbol appears in the play
- Uses specific, detailed examples from the text to support the analysis
- Makes clear connections to the text
- Properly integrates all quotations
- Organizes the information in a logical, easy-to-read manner
- Includes high-quality graphics that relate to the symbol and effectively enhance understanding of the topic
- Features clear and concise writing
- Uses correct spelling, grammar, and punctuation
- Clearly labels items of importance
- Headings and subheadings are clear and easy to read
- Uses layout to creatively enhances the information
- Creates a poster that is attractive in terms of layout, design, and organization
- Shows a strong effort by the student

# Symbolism in the Play

Symbolism is a literary technique that writers use to help propel the theme. A symbol can be a character, object, or event, which a writer uses to convey a deeper meaning. Action or dialogue in the narrative can also be symbolic of a specific idea or theme. When studying a work of literature, the reader can gain a deeper understanding of the story by identifying and analyzing the symbols. Symbolism may foreshadow events, and it can give the play's events, characters, and themes a universal feel. Sometimes, it sheds light on how the writer feels about specific concepts and ideas.

### The Storm

"Are not you moved when all the sway of earth
Shakes like a thing unfirm? O Cicero,
I have seen tempests when the scolding winds
Have rived the knotty oaks, and I have seen
Th' ambitious ocean swell and rage and foam
To be exalted with the threatening clouds,
But never till tonight, never till now,
Did I go through a tempest dropping fire.
Either there is a civil strife in heaven,
Or else the world, too saucy with the gods,
Incenses them to send destruction."

Casca, Act 1, Scene 3

**Casca**

## The Storm as a Symbol

The unusually turbulent storm can be interpreted as a symbol of the discord in Rome, due to Caesar's growing power, and the resulting conflict that will take place as Rome moves from being a republic to an empire. The storm can also be seen as a symbol of Brutus's struggle with his loyalty to Caesar versus his duty to the Republic of Rome. For Casca, the storm is a sign of the gods' displeasure, and Cassius sees the storm as a warning that the Romans must take action before Caesar is crowned emperor. For Calpurnia, the storm is an omen that her husband's life is in danger.

## Who Is Tied to the Storm?

## Other Symbols in the Play

### Feathers

Statues decorated with tributes to Caesar show his growing power. In Act 1, government officials Flavius and Marullus compare the decorations to feathers. In this case, feathers represent Caesar's ambition. The officials want to stop Caesar's rise and curb public support for him by removing the decorations on the statues. They compare their actions to plucking feathers from a bird to prevent it from flying higher.

### Crown

The crown is a symbol of royalty and power. In Act 1, when the crowd is celebrating Caesar's victory, Mark Antony offers Caesar a wreath of laurel leaves. The leaf crown represents power, but Caesar refuses it three times to demonstrate to the public that his intentions are **honorable**.

### Ghost

In the play, the ghost is a symbol that something terrible shall soon come to pass. When Brutus sees the ghost of Caesar, it is an omen of his own death. The ghost tells Brutus that he will see him again at Philippi. Brutus kills himself at Phillippi after his forces are defeated by Antony's army.

**TEACHER NOTES**

### More

**Who Is Tied to the Storm?**
Assess the author's use of symbolism in the play.

1. Choose a character from the chart and analyze what the symbol of the storm represents to him. For which character is this symbol the most poignant in the play? For which character is the symbol least poignant? Argue your opinions with clear reasons.
2. How is this symbol used or reflected in the play's themes? Illustrate the ways in which the author's use of language deepens or weakens the meaning of the storm as a symbol. Explain and defend your ideas.

### Weblink

***Julius Caesar*: Ghosts and Spirits**
Examine the article about ghosts and spirits in *Julius Caesar*.

1. Shakespeare is well known for featuring ghosts in his plays. Why do you think there are more references to ghosts and spirits in *Julius Caesar* than in any other Shakespearean play? What is the significance of this?
2. What particular commentary might the author be making about life as a result of this theme's presence in the text? Explain and defend your ideas.

# The Use of Language

Shakespeare began composing his works when the English language was relatively young. He wrote approximately 37 plays, 2 narrative poems, and 154 sonnets. Shakespeare experimented with English by creating new words and phrases, and scholars attribute thousands of words and many expressions to him. Some of these new words were created by combining two words together. Shakespeare's influence on the English language shapes the way people speak and write today. Without Shakespeare, there would not be phrases such as "in a pickle," or "love is blind." Here are some words and phrases that appear in the works of Shakespeare.

## Prose and Poetry

The two principal categories of literature are prose and poetry. Prose is the spoken or written language that people use every day. Poetry may also be spoken or written, but it tends to be more expressive, and uses elements such as rhyme and rhythm. Poems also tend to be structured with ideas contained in lines and verses, while prose expresses ideas in sentences. Shakespeare used prose and verse to indicate the social status of his characters, with those of a higher status speaking in verse and those of a lower status speaking in prose.

The lines of a poem can be divided into a rhythmic unit called a poetic foot. A poetic foot uses a combination of stressed and unstressed syllables, which create a unit of rhythm, or meter. Writers of English verse use four primary poetic feet called anapestic, trochaic, dactylic, and iambic.

## Iambic Pentameter

When Shakespeare composed his plays in the late sixteenth and early seventeenth centuries, storytellers commonly used poetry. Shakespeare predominantly composed his plays using iambic pentameter. This poetic meter allowed him the flexibility to express the subtlety and rhythms of everyday speech. Iambic pentameter is a unit of verse with a specific poetic foot and line length. Each foot is made of two syllables. The first syllable is unstressed and the second is stressed. The rhythm of each line follows a specific sound pattern.

Verse written in iambic pentameter is usually divided into five feet per line, with ten syllables in total. Iambic pentameter can be used in both formal and rhyming poetry. It can also be used in blank verse, which does not rhyme, but follows a meter.

In Act 1, Scene 1 of *Julius Caesar*, Flavius meets a group of revelers and demands to know the occupation of one of the men. Read aloud with the rhythmic pattern of iambic pentameter, the stressed syllables in this line are as follows:

What **trade**, thou **knave**? Thou **naugh**ty **knave**, what **trade**?

In the same scene, Marullus criticizes the cobbler for celebrating Caesar's triumph. When this line is read aloud with a rhythmic pattern of iambic pentameter, the stressed syllables are as follows:

You **blocks**, you **stones**, you **worse** than **sense**less **things**!

### TEACHER NOTES

#### Video

**Why Shakespeare loved iambic pentameter - David T. Freeman and Gregory Taylor**

Learn more about Shakespeare's use of language by watching this video.

1. Why do you think Shakespeare's words have such staying power? Explain how Shakespeare's use of rhythm connects to the way people spoke in his time and the way people still speak today.
2. In what situations do Shakespeare's characters typically turn to poetry? Why? What is the significance of this switch to iambic pentameter?

#### Weblink

***The Difference Between Poetry and Prose***

Learn more about poetry and prose in this blog post.

1. Compare and contrast poetry and prose. In what ways are they similar? How are they different? What stance, if any, does the blogger take?
2. The blogger claims that "prose is principally an ethical project," whereas "poetry is amoral." What does he mean by this? Do you agree with this assertion? Why or why not?

**EXTENSION ACTIVITY**

### Holding a Classroom Debate

**Students will form groups and prepare arguments for a debate on a controversial issue. Exemplary performance in a debate will meet the following criteria.**

- Demonstrates in-depth understanding of the topic and related information
- Presents strong, logical, and convincing arguments
- Communicates in a clear and confident manner
- Maintains eye contact
- Uses clear vocal tone and a reasonable rate of vocal delivery
- Uses respectful and appropriate language and body language
- Delivers arguments, evidence, and counter-evidence in an engaging and persuasive manner
- Supports each major point of an argument with several relevant and detailed facts and examples
- Connects all arguments to the overall topic in a clear, concise, and organized manner
- Presents the arguments and supporting evidence in a clear, logical manner
- Presents clear, thorough, and accurate information throughout the debate
- Addresses all of the opposing team's arguments with counter-arguments
- Identifies any weakness in the opposing team's arguments
- Constructs strong and relevant counter-arguments using accurate information
- Presents strong and persuasive arguments throughout the debate
- Summarizes the arguments in the closing statement

# Impact of the Play when First Performed

Plays based on historical events and characters were popular when *Julius Caesar* debuted in 1599. The Elizabethan public would have been familiar with the story of Julius Caesar and known that he had twice invaded Britain. Some of the audience may even have read the English translation of *Lives of Noble Grecians and Romans* by the Greek biographer Plutarch, which Shakespeare used as a resource. People were concerned for the future after Queen Elizabeth I's death. It was unclear who would succeed her, since the Queen did not have an heir. There had also been uprisings, threats of assassinations, and attempts to overthrow her.

## An Early Critic

Thomas Platter, a Swiss tourist, made the earliest critique of *Julius Caesar*. Platter saw the play on September 21, 1599, and wrote in his diary, "...witnessed an excellent performance of the tragedy of the first Emperor Julius Caesar with a cast of some fifteen people; when the play was over, they danced very marvelously and gracefully together..."

## Friend and Rival

*Poet and playwright Ben Jonson was a contemporary of Shakespeare. Jonson found fault with several lines from Julius Caesar, accusing Shakespeare of sloppiness. Jonson may have been jealous of Shakespeare, as the play was a success, and his own Roman play was a failure. After Shakespeare's death, however, Jonson wrote that Shakespeare was a great playwright whose works would live on forever.*

## First Folio

In 1616, seven years after Shakespeare's death, 36 of his plays were collected into one volume. The book, published in 1623, is now called the *First Folio*. Of these plays, 18 had never been published before. The *First Folio* is considered extremely important. Without it, some of Shakespeare's most famous works, such as *The Tragedy of Julius Caesar,* may not have been preserved. Today, there are only 235 surviving copies of the *First Folio*.

# Reputation

*Shakespeare had many* ***patrons****, including King James I. This support meant all members of Shakespeare's company could call themselves gentlemen. The company was also protected from the Puritans, a group of Protestants who believed theater was a corrupting influence. The King's support allowed Shakespeare a degree of financial security. While Shakespeare was considered successful, his reputation as an outstanding playwright was not established until the eighteenth century.*

# Generating Discussions

Within a year of *Julius Caesar*'s debut, the Globe had become a successful theater. The play voiced political ideas that could not be expressed elsewhere, due to strict Elizabethan censorship laws. Themes of power, corruption, and loyalty remained relevant, and in later years, *Julius Caesar* gained popularity with audiences in the United States. American audiences drew parallels between the overthrow of Caesar and the American fight for independence from British rule.

## TEACHER NOTES

### Video

**The *First Folio*: A 400 Year Obsession**

Discover how the *First Folio* has inspired its devotees for hundreds of years by watching this video.

1. Why do you think so many people have tried to associate themselves with the *First Folio* over the years? What is the appeal of the book? How does it continue to inspire creativity today?
2. Why would a serious study of the *First Folio* require collecting multiple copies in one place? What can be learned about Shakespeare and his works by comparing different copies of the *First Folio*?

### Weblink

**Ben Jonson**

Find out more about Ben Jonson by reviewing this biography.

1. Jonson is said to have been both Shakespeare's friend and his rival. What are the advantages of such a relationship? Can you think of any disadvantages?
2. The article says that, "[u]nlike Shakespeare, Jonson gives a distorted or incomplete picture of life." How do you think Shakespeare accomplishes this complete picture of life in his works? Give examples from *Julius Caesar*.

**EXTENSION ACTIVITY**

### Writing a Review

**Students will write a review of the play. An exemplary review will meet the following criteria.**

- Grabs the reader's attention with a creative headline
- Begins with an engaging lead to pull the reader into the article
- Introduces the title of the play, the author, and the genre
- Provides a brief plot description that does not give away the entire story, and makes the reader want to learn more about the play
- Supports arguments about the play with accurate and detailed information
- Organizes the review and its arguments in a concise, clear, and logical manner
- Fits the format and style of a review
- Follows the conventions of print or online journalism
- Demonstrates creativity in their approach
- Writes with a unique, engaging voice and perspective
- Provides fresh insight into the play
- Provides an honest, authentic opinion on the play
- Gives a clear recommendation on the play, backed up by specific textual evidence
- Uses correct spelling, grammar, and punctuation

# Impact of the Play Now

*The Tragedy of Julius Caesar*, written more than 400 years ago, is still exciting and relevant. The play is often part of modern discussions on politics, due to its timeless themes of power, corruption, and betrayal. The text is discussed by actors, students, scholars, and the public, and the play is staged at theaters and festivals all over the world. It has featured all-female casts, been set on the African continent, and rewritten into street slang with hip hop beats. Artists continue to be inspired by *Julius Caesar* to create new novels, parodies, music, or manga.

Shakespeare's work has been **translated** into more than **100 languages**.

## Shakespeare's Birthplace

Stratford-upon-Avon, England, promotes Shakespeare's legacy through restored properties connected to the playwright. These include his wife Anne Hathaway's cottage, his mother's childhood farm, and his schoolroom. A new exhibition features contemporary landscapes where Shakespeare's home originally stood. There are nine sculptures in the garden, representing nine of Shakespeare's plays, including *Julius Caesar*.

## The Globe

The Puritans began closing theaters in 1642. The Globe was destroyed two years later. In 1970, an American actor named Sam Wanamaker started the Shakespeare Globe Trust to raise the necessary funds and secure a property to rebuild the Globe. As there was no exact plan of the original Globe, architects incorporated written accounts, illustrations, and designs of existing buildings from the period into the new building. Wanamaker worked for more than two decades on the project. He died in 1993 in London before it came to completion. In June 1997, the Queen reopened the Globe, and it remains immensely popular today.

## Shakespeare 400

In 2016, events were held around the world to celebrate the 400th anniversary of Shakespeare's death. One exhibit, entitled "Shakespeare's Here and Everywhere," used maps to explore how Shakespeare and his audiences imagined foreign places, including Ancient Rome. As part of the celebration, BBC's Radio 4 launched a new production of *Julius Caesar*.

## Folger Shakespeare Library

The Folger, in Washington, D.C., has the world's largest collection of Shakespeare's work. The first play ever produced for the library's stage was a 1949 production of *Julius Caesar*, which used text from the *First Folio*. That same year, their performance became the first nationally broadcast Shakespearean play. In 2016, the Folger, along with the Cincinnati Museum Center and the American Library Association, launched an exhibition of the *First Folio*. As part of the tour, Amherst College held a screening of the 1949 production.

### TEACHER NOTES

#### Document

***Julius Caesar* review – political thriller chimes with rise of populism**

Examine the review by Catherine Love, published on May 25, 2017, of Robert Hastie's production of *Julius Caesar*.

1. Do you think that Love gives an honest, authentic opinion on the production? Why or why not? Cite evidence from the review to support your position.
2. Who is the intended audience for this play? Based on this review, do you think the play is appropriate for this target audience? Give reasons for your answer. Who would you recommend this performance to and why?

#### Weblink

**Globe Theatre**

Discover more about the success, design, and history of the Globe in this article.

1. Why did Shakespeare's company build the Globe? How successful was the theater? Why do you think this is?
2. The article claims that "[t]he basic justification for attempting to reconstruct the Globe in a faithful version of the original is that it can be used to learn more about Shakespeare's plays." Do you think this is true, and if so, how? Explain your answer.

**EXTENSION ACTIVITY**

## Creating a Timeline

**Students will explore a topic related to the play and create a timeline to present their research on historical events connected to this topic. An exemplary timeline will meet the following criteria.**

- Includes the most significant events pertaining to the topic to be compared and analyzed
- Includes interesting events
- Uses accurate information for all events, including date, location, and major details
- Orders the events in a chronological sequence
- Describes each event with accurate, vivid, and specific details
- Presents the topic from three or more perspectives
- Inspires the reader to ask thoughtful questions regarding the events and perspectives presented in the timeline
- Uses correct spelling, grammar, and punctuation
- Presents the timeline in a visually attractive and striking manner
- Presents the timeline in a neat, organized manner that is logical and easy to follow
- Uses creativity to present the timeline in an engaging manner
- Effectively communicates the historical information relating to the topic
- Supports each event with reliable sources
- Expresses a clear purpose for creating the timeline
- Enhances the reader's understanding of the topic
- Includes a correctly formatted bibliography of all sources used to create the timeline

# The Roman Republic and American Independence

Shakespeare's *The Tragedy of Julius Caesar* explores political ambition and the consequences of political change. After Caesar is assassinated, Rome slips into civil war. The event that Brutus and Cassius had been trying to prevent occurs with the end of the Republic. The actual Roman Republic began in 509 BC. This is when the Romans overthrew their last king, Lucius Tarquinius Superbus. The people of Rome established a new system of government, in which power was to be shared by several bodies to prevent one person from gaining control.

## Timeline

### Political Acts

**1763** After the Seven Year's War (1756–1763) ends with the signing of the Treaty of Paris, King George III issues a proclamation forbidding settlement past the Appalachian Mountains.

**1765** The British Parliament passes the Stamp Act, which levies taxes on colonists in an attempt to finance the costs of protecting the American colonies.

**1768** British troops occupy Boston to enforce the unpopular Townshend duties on products such as a tea or paper.

**1760s**

### Social Effects

**1760s** American Colonists argue against British-imposed taxes with the slogan, "No taxation without representation."

**1770** A group of Boston citizens clash with British soldiers who open fire in what came to be known as the Boston Massacre.

**1773** American Patriots dump tea belonging to the East India Tea Company into Boston Harbor after the British Government imposes the Tea Act. This Act gives the East India Company a monopoly over the sale of tea in the colonies.

In the first century BC, Rome's power still lay with its senators, but infighting caused the government to be unstable. In 60 BC, Gaius Julius Caesar rose to power. He later seized control. After his murder in 44 BC, the Republic became an Empire. The ideas of the Roman Republic did not end with Rome's fall. They inspired the founders of the United States when they were creating the new nation. In the Declaration of Independence, Thomas Jefferson wrote, "We hold these truths to be self-evident: that all men are created equal; that they are endowed by their Creator with certain unalienable rights; that among these are life, liberty, and the pursuit of happiness."

**1775** The first shots of the American Revolutionary War are fired at Lexington and Concord, which lead to the first major battle, the Battle of Bunker Hill.

**1774** To punish the American colonists, the British Parliament passes the Coercive Acts, which colonists call the Intolerable Acts.

**1770s**

**1774** Defiant Colonists boycott British goods, and colonial delegates meet at the first Continental Congress to discuss opposition to the Intolerable Acts.

**1776** American colonists declare their independence with the adoption of the Declaration of Independence by the Continental Congress.

**1775** The Continental Congress appoints George Washington leader of the Revolutionary forces.

## TEACHER NOTES

### Transparency–Timeline

**Timeline of Political Acts and Social Effects**

Examine the historical and cultural contexts shown on the timeline. Then, contrast and correlate its elements with the themes and events presented in *Julius Caesar.*

1. In what ways can historical events, culture, and social mores influence a population's perspective on political acts and their social effects? How might these elements have shaped the way a reader in the late 1590s or early 1600s interpreted the play?
2. How might the era in which William Shakespeare wrote *Julius Caesar* have influenced the play's themes and settings? Where in the play is this most evident? Explain your reasoning.
3. Which current events, changes in laws, new ideas, or political discussions are shaping the future of the United States? Which ideas and attitudes are still prevailing? Why?
4. How might current events and present perspectives affect the way a reader interprets the play? Why is it important for readers to understand the era and context in which a play is written?

**EXTENSION ACTIVITY**

### Writing a Comparative Essay

**Students will compare two literary devices used in the play, and then write a comparative essay based on their analysis. An exemplary comparative essay will meet the following criteria.**

- Consists of a one-paragraph introduction, three body paragraphs, and a one-paragraph conclusion
- Introduction includes an engaging lead statement about the topic of the essay, more detailed information about the play, and a one-sentence thesis that specifically states the essay's argument
- Body paragraphs include a topic sentence that refers to the thesis and how the idea appears in the play, a supporting sentence that points to this part of the play, textual evidence of this idea from the play, and analysis of this evidence
- Body paragraphs end with a transition to the next paragraph
- Conclusion refers to the topic of the essay and the three points presented in the body paragraphs, and restates the thesis
- Provides a thorough analysis of the literary devices in question
- Cites strong and thorough textual evidence to support analysis of what the play says explicitly
- Presents a clear, specific thesis that indicates a high level of critical engagement
- Organizes ideas in a logical manner
- Communicates arguments in a clear, effective manner
- Properly integrates all quotations
- Correctly cites all sources used
- Correctly formats bibliography

# Writing a Comparative Essay

*The Tragedy of Julius Caesar* is brought to life with carefully drawn characters, dynamic verse, and vivid prose, through themes of power and corruption, loyalty, and betrayal. After studying the play, write a comparative essay exploring how two literary devices are used in *Julius Caesar*. This could be a comparison of characters, themes, symbols, or settings. To write a comparative essay, you will need to formulate an argument. Your argument should clearly state how your compared elements are similar or different. Support your argument with valid reasoning and evidence from the play.

## How to Analyze and Compare Characters

Use the chart to guide your comparison of two characters in *Julius Caesar*.

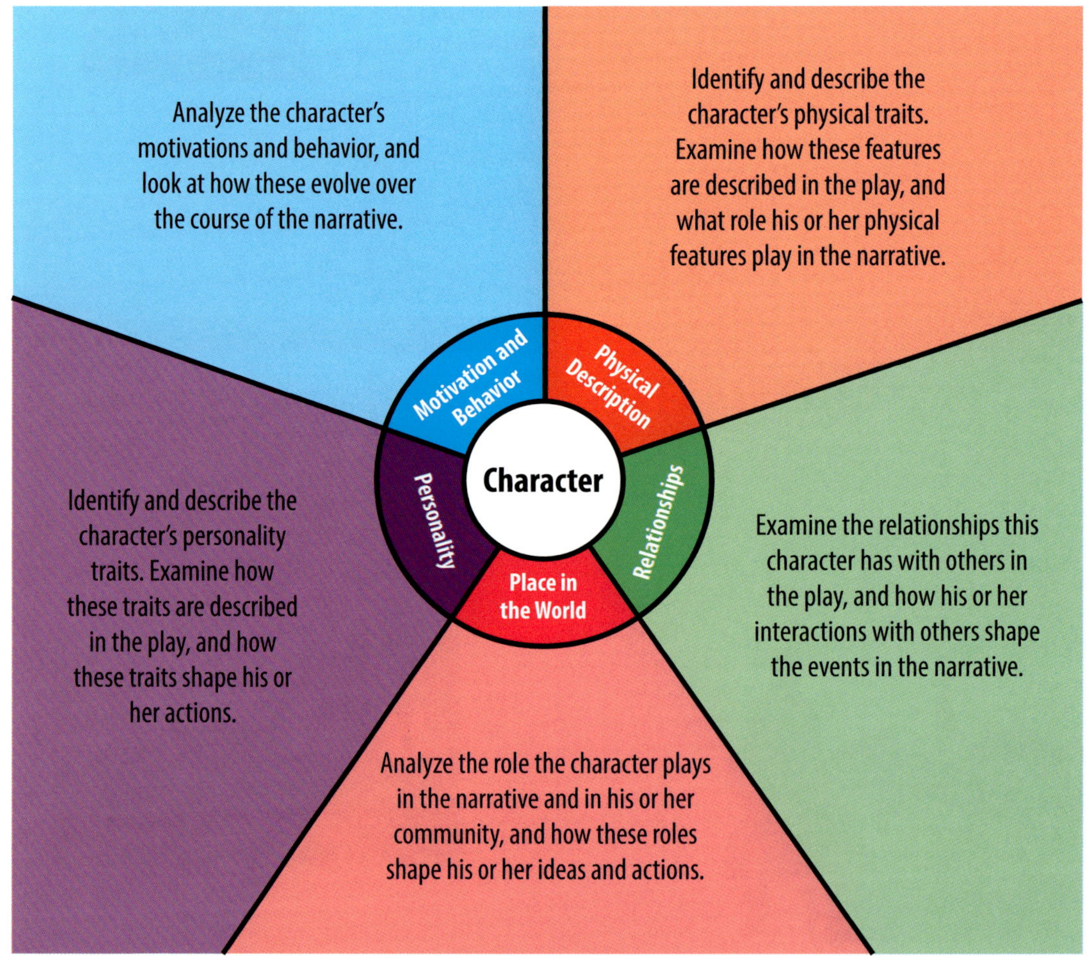

## Comparing Marcus Brutus and Julius Caesar

### Marcus Brutus

**Personality**
- Noble
- Patriotic
- Impractical
- Idealistic

**Motivation and Behavior**
- Wants to be honorable
- Champions the cause of the Republic
- Is suspicious of Caesar
- Attempts to rein in the violence

**Place in the World**
- The protagonist of the play
- A respected member of Roman society
- Feels he needs to protect the freedom of the Roman people
- A tragic hero who commits murder

**Relationships**
- A Roman senator
- Married to Portia
- Was a friend of Caesar's
- Kind master to his servants
- Respected by other Roman citizens and Senators

**Physical Description**
- Eloquent speaker
- Wears a toga
- A strong soldier

### Julius Caesar

**Place in the World**
- Has many enemies
- Plays an important role as leader of Rome
- Feels invincible

**Physical Description**
- Deaf
- Weak
- Compares himself to the Northern Star

**Motivation and Behavior**
- Acts according to what he believes the people expect of him
- Works to rule the Roman Empire directly
- Wants to be respected
- Responds to threats by showing no fear

**Relationships**
- Husband to Calpurnia
- Soldier and ruler of Rome
- Authoritative ruler
- Is compared to a tyrant

**Personality**
- Proud
- Ambitious
- Strong
- Arrogant

## TEACHER NOTES

### Transparency–Chart

**Questions for Character Analysis**

Analyze how specific character features, such as conflicts, motivations, relationships, place in the world, and personality affect the plot of *Julius Caesar*. Cite strong and thorough textual evidence to support your analysis of what the play says explicitly as well as the inferences you may have drawn from the play's setting, themes, and symbols.

### Quiz Answers

1. D
2. B
3. B
4. A
5. C
6. C
7. D
8. A
9. D
10. B

# Key Words

**ambition:** the desire to strive or want to achieve, as in power, fame, or riches

**betray:** to deceive or disappoint the expectations of someone close

**conspiracy:** when a group of people meet secretly to plan an evil act

**corrupt:** dishonest and disloyal

**honorable:** being committed to one's beliefs and actions

**influence:** the action or power to produce a change in another

**loyalty:** a certain point of view or position regarding a subject

**manipulated:** changed the behavior of another

**patrons:** people with the power to give financial or other kinds of support

**rhetoric:** to use language effectively, often influencing people through a speech

**values:** an individual's standards of behavior and what aspects of life they consider to be most important

# Literary Terms

**act:** a division in a play made up of scenes that contain elements such as rising action

**action:** everything that occurs in a narrative

**antagonist:** the character who stands in opposition to the protagonist; in some cases, the antagonist creates or represents the conflict that the protagonist faces

**bibliography:** a list of sources used in a written work

**characterization:** how the author reveals a character's personality

**climax:** the moment of greatest tension in the story's action

**conflict:** a struggle between two or more opposing forces, creating a tension that must be resolved

**dialogue:** the spoken conversations that the characters have with each other

**exposition:** the beginning of the story, where the characters and setting are introduced

**falling action:** the events that take place after the climax, leading up to the end of the story

**Freytag's Pyramid:** a narrative structure consisting of five elements; this includes exposition, rising action, climax, falling action, and resolution

**internal dialogue:** a conversation that a character has with him or herself, or what a character is thinking

**mood:** the overall feeling that the narrative is intended to evoke within the reader

**narrative:** a logically arranged series of events presented for an audience; a story

**narrator:** the character or person telling the story, providing background information and opinions on the events, and connecting the gaps between major events and dialogue

**plot:** the specific action that propels a story forward

**protagonist:** the central character in a piece of fiction, who must deal with a conflict, and often undergoes some change as a result

**resolution:** the end of the story, when the problems are resolved, and the action comes to a conclusion

**rising action:** the events that create increased drama or tension

**sonnets:** poems with 14 lines, with each line having 10 syllables

**style:** the unique way that writers use language to tell their story; this can include word choice, the use of imagery, and the length and organization of sentences

**symbolism:** a literary technique using symbols to represent and intensify concepts and ideas

**theme:** the underlying topic, idea, or position in a work that is often a general, universal statement about life

**tragedy:** a type of drama that deals with a serious subject

# Index

# LIGHTBOX

## SUPPLEMENTARY RESOURCES

Click on the plus icon found in the bottom left corner of each spread to open additional teacher resources.

- Download and print the book's quizzes and activities
- Access curriculum correlations
- Explore additional web applications that enhance the Lightbox experience

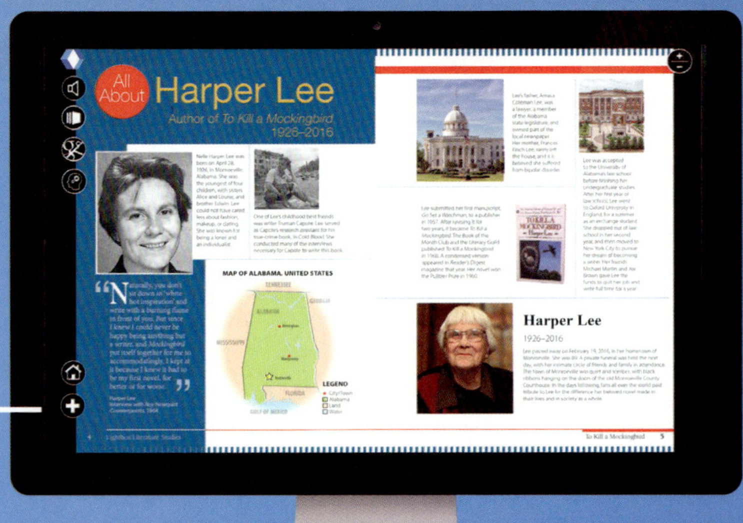


## LIGHTBOX DIGITAL TITLES
### Packed full of integrated media

**VIDEOS**

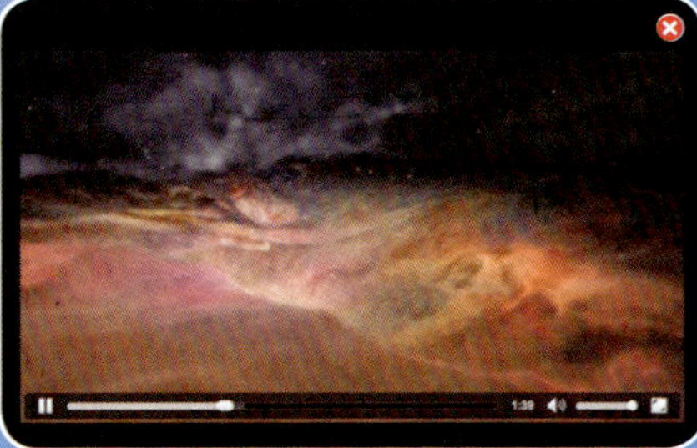

**INTERACTIVE MAPS**

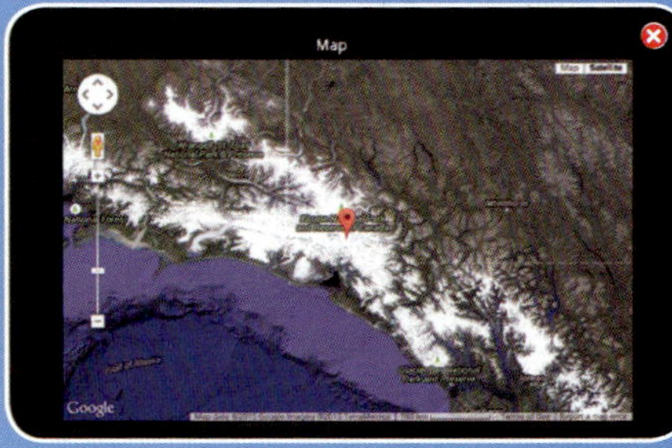


**WEBLINKS**

**SLIDESHOWS**

**QUIZZES**

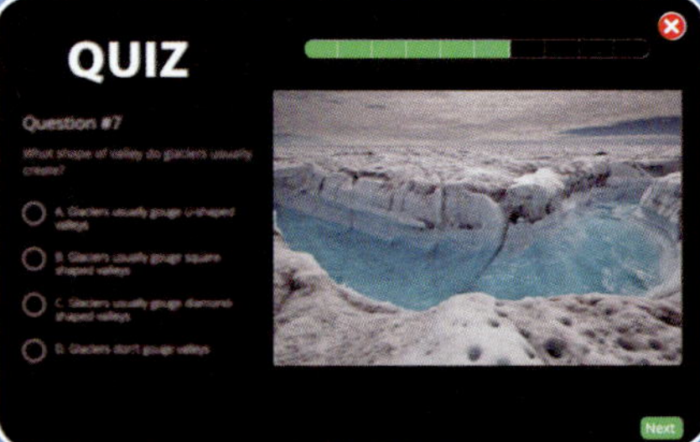


**OPTIMIZED FOR**

- ✔ TABLETS
- ✔ WHITEBOARDS
- ✔ COMPUTERS
- ✔ AND MUCH MORE!


Published by Smartbook Media Inc.
350 5th Avenue, 59th Floor New York, NY 10118
Website: www.openlightbox.com





Library of Congress Cataloging-in-Publication Data

Names: Yasuda, Anita, author.
Title: Julius Caesar / Anita Yasuda.
Description: New York, NY : Smartbook Media Inc., [2018] | Series: Lightbox literature studies | Includes index.
Identifiers: LCCN 2016051609 (print) | LCCN 2017006301 (ebook) | ISBN 9781510519978 (hard cover : alk. paper) | ISBN 9781510519985 (multi-user ebk.)
Subjects: LCSH: Shakespeare, William, 1564-1616. Julius Caesar--Examinations--Study guides. | Caesar, Julius--In literature. | Assassination in literature. | Conspiracies in literature. | Tragedy. | Rome--In literature.
Classification: LCC PR2808 .Y37 2017 (print) | LCC PR2808 (ebook) | DDC 822.3/3--dc23
LC record available at https://lccn.loc.gov/2016051609

Printed in Brainerd, Minnesota, United States
1 2 3 4 5 6 7 8 9 0 21 20 19 18 17

062017
042017

**Editor:** Katie Gillespie
**Art Director:** Terry Paulhus

Every reasonable effort has been made to trace ownership and to obtain permission to reprint copyright material. The publisher would be pleased to have any errors or omissions brought to its attention so that they may be corrected in subsequent printings.

The publisher acknowledges Getty Images, Alamy, iStock, and Wikimedia Commons as its primary image suppliers for this title.